"BUDGETING AS A TOOL FOR ENHANCING FINANCIAL MANAGEMENT IN LOCAL GOVERNMENT AUTHORITIES, ADA EAST DISTRICT ASSEMBLY AS A STUDY

Dr. David Ackah - UM27358BEC35586 / UD30576BEC39151
Ph.D. /M.Phil. / MSc (Economics)
Atlantic International University – AIU, Hawaii, Honolulu, U.S.A
Department of Business & Economics
drdavidackah@gmail.com / david.ackah@gmail.com

Makafui R. Agboyi – COVSCM0910010
MSc Supply Chain Management / MCIPS
Conventry University, United Kingdom
Faculty of Engineering & Computing
makafuiagboyi@gmail.com

I0484520

ABSTRACT

MMDAs as development partners to the central government need to mobilize enough revenue locally to support the central government development agenda. Inadequate financial resources can undermine the effective implementation of developmental projects in MMDAs. Budgets are important as they prudently manage scarce financial resources and at the same time serve as a means of expenditure authorization, control and evaluation base. MMDAs in Ghana, prepare budgets but deal with it in lesser extent, unlike the profit-making organizations which consider budget and budgetary controls important element in their policies. It is against this background that this study was carried out to find ways by which MMDAS especially AEDA can use budgeting and budgetary controls as management tools to prudently enhance their financial management system for local development. The case study approach was used in the study. Interviews and questionnaires were used to solicit data for the study.

The research found out among other things that MMDAs prepare budgets and control the budgets. The research data evidently prove that in the case of Ada East District Assembly, this is true. However, poor budget formulation and implementation and low revenue generation base make it difficult for MMDAs to live up to their responsibility as partners to the central government in national development. Recommendations and suggestions have accordingly been made to improve upon budgeting and budgetary controls in MMDAs and the nation as a whole.

Key Word: "Budgeting As A Tool For Enhancing Financial Management In Local Government Authorities

Introduction

Central governments over the world have made human and environmental development their primary objective and have therefore used decentralization as a method of sharing development responsibilities with Para-state agencies such as the local authorities. Rodinell (1981) defines decentralization as the transfer of authority to plan, make decisions and manage public funds and functions from a higher level of government to individuals, organizations or agencies at lower level. Aryee (1999) identifies four forms of decentralization.

These are administrative, economic, political and fiscal. Local government in Ghana, especially Metropolitan, Municipal and District Assemblies (MMDAs) were established with the sole aim of generating good contacts with the citizens and to bring decision making to the level where development generally takes place. MMDAs were also created to help strengthen the democratic process and lay the basis for the upsurge of autonomous institutions of governance within the structure of the nation-state. According to Aryee and Amponsah (2003), the District Assemblies have added potential advantage such as spreading development skills throughout the society.

To ensure development, the government of Ghana in 1988 promulgated a local government law, Provisional National Defense Council (PNDC) Law 207 to establish one hundred and ten (110) local authorities. Sections 241 of the 1992 constitution and local Government Act 462 (1993) have been the basis for the adoption of the current decentralization program in Ghana. Currently, the number of MMDAs has increase to 216 with 55 as Municipal and 6 as Metropolitan Assemblies. There are massive responsibilities, spelt out in Act 462 specifying the functions and responsibilities of the District Assemblies in Ghana. The Local Government Act 462 (1993) Section 10, sub -section 3 states that the Districts Assemblies shall be responsible for the overall development of their district and preparation and submission of development plans. MMDAs are charged by the local government law with physical development responsibilities such as to:

1. Ensure legal arbitration;
2. Register birth, death marriage and divorce;
3. Give building permits to ensure proper spatial development;
4. Build schools, provide books and furniture;
5. Maintain law and order;
6. Establish and maintain parks and gardens;
7. Provide street lights;
8. Provide health, sanitation and waste management service;
9. Provide social services;
10. Provide firefighting services;
11. Provide markets;

(Local Government Act, Act 462 (1993)

MMDAs are charged by various enactments including the 1992 Constitution to ensure physical transformation of the various local areas and stimulate socio-economic activities and development so as to change civic inertia, poverty and illiteracy to enhance equity, efficiency, effectiveness and economy in their entrepreneurship. These functions of the MMDAs cannot be achieved without adequate financial resources to support them.

Inadequate financial resources can undermine the effective implementation of developmental projects in the districts. It is against this background that the new Local Government System has made provision for the financing of the districts.

Fiscal decentralization is the transfer of responsibilities, power and resources to lower level public authority to mobilize funds for development that is autonomous and fully independent from the devolving authority when narrowed down to devolution. Local authorities are given responsibilities and financial means within the national level determining the scope and quality of services to be provided and amount of funds needed to deliver these services. Kessey and Diaw (2002) called for vigorous revenue mobilization drive if the MMDAs are to perform better. They mention that the effectiveness of revenue mobilization depends on factors such as fiscal policy, revenue administration, monitoring operations and performance assessments. Unfortunately many MMDAs do not generate enough revenue. The reasons for their inability to mobilize enough revenue are numerous. To mention a few Kessey and Diaw (ibid) list corrupt practices, poor mobilization strategies, poor budget control and poor financial management as the major reasons. Prudent financial management refers to how wisely resources are mobilized and managed effectively and efficiently. Financial management is therefore an important aspect of public administration of every nation and it is one of the elements that make government effective. It involves financial forecasting, financial planning and budgeting, financial reporting and auditing. Sound financial management is one of the important complements of effective management practices which seek to enhance the socio-economic development of local authorities in Ghana. Marshall and Synder (1974) stress that in order to ensure sound financial management there should be good planning, accounting and budgetary systems.

Jackson (1958) states that without financial independence, local authorities must lead a very subdued life. Therefore funds should be mobilized from taxes levied on citizens and residents within the territories of the local authorities. Officials must spend funds in a manner governed by rules and regulations. Currently good financial management is being used by donors as a precedent for debt relief such as HIPC, GSOP and other financial assistance to developing countries.

ABOUT THE PROBLEM

MMDAs as development partners to the central government need to generate sufficient revenue locally to support the central government development agenda. Budgets are necessary to prudently manage scarce financial resources and at the same time serve as means of expenditure authorization, control and evaluation base. Profit making organizations consider budget and budgetary controls as important elements in their policy making.

The success of their organizations depends largely on good budget preparation and effective budgetary controls. In Ghana, MMDAs prepare budgets but the degree and extent to which budgets are prepared and formulated into performance budgets vary from each other. Even where formal budgets are prepared their nature and purposes may vary. Failure of many businesses nowadays erupt from the fact that budgets and budgetary controls which are the bedrock of any successful business organizations is weak or absent as reported by Ministry of Health, (1977) and Bradstreet, (2004). Such organizations or businesses are characterized by financial, administrative, production, managerial etc. constraints. Budgets should be prepared based on availability of resources. MMDAs should ensure that they generate enough resources to compliment central government grants which are always inadequate. They can also look elsewhere for resources to support their budgets.

It means some activities captured in the budget could not be undertaken or part touched. Ada East District Assembly prepares budget but most times the expenditure always exceeds the revenue resulting in budget deficits. It does not mean that budgets are ideal manager's tool. This observation encourages numerous academicians to try to discover appropriate solutions for budget slacking, budget gamming, budget bias and other problems that managers had to deal with, Harper (1995). In line with this argument, the study looks at whether; MMDAs in Ghana can achieve their objectives with or without effective budget and budgetary control systems. It is to find out reasons for budget failure and deficits at Ada East District Assembly where budgetary control is cited as a cause for poor performance in development process.

The problem is that most MMDAs do not have effective financial control system due to poor budget formulation and implementation. They experience budget deficits which normally occur because:

a. There is poor data base for planning and budgeting;
b. There is poor budgetary control resulting in embezzlements, misappropriations and misapplication of funds culminating in over expenditures;
c. There is lack of ownership and responsibility when it comes to budgetary control. Poor data base for planning and budgeting also have other consequences. The consequences are that:

i) Revenues may be over-estimated to the extent that the estimated revenue is higher than the actual revenue;
ii) Expenditures may be under-estimated to the extent that the actual expenditure is higher than the estimated expenditure.

Some other rate and property rate payers may fail to fulfill their legitimate obligations in rate payment. This may also result in situations where actual revenue may be lower than the estimated revenue. Revenue deficits may also occur as a result of dishonesty of revenue collectors. While useful revenue cannot be collected, expenditures go on without adequate controls resulting in excess expenditures over-revenue. When these happen MMDAs cannot live up to their responsibility of being partners to the central government in the development effort. The citizens are also denied facilities and economic services for their business take offs.

LITERATURE REVIEW
CONCEPT OF MANAGEMENT CONTROL

The literature holds a large number of definitions of management control. The modern management control system originated with the influential work of Robert Anthony (1965) who drew boundaries between management control, strategic planning and operation control. He recognizes accounting language as the base for commonalities in the system. Anthony (Ibid) defines management control as the processes by which managers assure that resources are obtained and used efficiently in the accomplishment of the organization's objectives" Garrison and Noreen (2000) suggest a different definition of management control as follows: "those steps taken by management that attempt to increase the likelihood that the objectives set down at the planning stage are attained and to ensure that all parts of the organization function in a manner consistent with organizational policies.

In this paper, the term management control is defined as those sets of organizational activities that include planning, coordination, communication, evaluation and decision-making as well as informal processes aimed at enhancing the efficient and effective use of the organizational resources towards the achievement of the organizational objectives. Budgeting is the tool used by management to facilitate those management activities. Anthony and Govindarajan (2004) identify several aspects or activities of management control namely, planning, coordinating, communication, evaluation, decision-making and influencing.

1. Planning what the organization should do. Planning could be viewed as budget preparation.
2. Coordinating the activities of several parts of the organization to assure alignments goals.

3. Communicating information such as strategy and specific performance objectives. Communication could be done formally (by means of budgets and other official documents) and informal through conversations.
4. Evaluating actual performance relative to the standard and making inferences as to how well the manager has performed.
5. Deciding what, if any action should be taken.

THE BUDGET

Over the past two decades, one word that has become the common currency in all managers' vocabulary is "budgets". The budget is perhaps the most chosen course of action or in action by the management and staff across all sectors. Management at all level within the public, private and the third sector have used the budget as their shield or excuse when confronted or challenged about any decision. It's not uncommon to hear variations of the phrases "the budget doesn't permit us to" or it's not our budget. Frederick (2001) and he defines budget as plan that is measurable and timely. Bruns and Waterhouse (1975) also define budget as financial plans that provide the basis for directing and evaluating the performance of individuals or segments of organizations. Merchant (1981) defines budgeting system as a combination of information flows and administrative processes and procedures that are usually integral part of the short-range planning and control system of an organization.

Drury (2006) defines budget as a plan expressed in quantitative, usually monetary term covering a specific period of time usually one year in other words a budget is a systematic plan for the utilization of manpower and materials resources. In a business organization a budget represents an estimate of future costs and revenues. Lucey (1996) defines budget as a plan expressed in money terms. It is prepared and approved prior to the budget and may show income, expenditure and the capital to be employed. It may be drawn up showing incremental effects of former budgeted or actual figures, or be compiled by zero - based budgeting.

Blocher et al (2002), argue that budgets help to allocate resources, coordinate operations and provide a means for performance measurement. MMDAs like other organizations undertake various forms of policies, programs and activities covering economic, social, political etc. These activities entail financial counterpart in the form of revenue and expenditure. MMDAs document these intensions and their related financial implication in the form of a plan. Oduro (2006) mentions that such a plan backing the local authorities are intended actions and a program for the forthcoming period usually a year. It is called a budget. A budget is a document that reflects the estimates of income and expenditure of a government, local authority or a firm for a particular period of time, possibly, from 1st January to 31st December.

Some objectives are realized in the short-term and some are realized in the long- term in relation to multi-year programs that have been adopted, Erasmus and Visser (2000) state that an annual budget thus serves as an implementation tool for long-term objectives.

Public sector budget, according to Oduro (Ibid) is a prospectus referring to expected future revenue and expenditure activities of the government for the forthcoming period. It is used as an instrument to allocate public resources toward achieving some public value.

Budgets, by definition, have to be prepared in advance and for this reason, they are often referred to in terms of their being part of a feed forward system. Feedback is a term frequently heard both in accounting and ordinary use. According to Hall (1996) feed forward, on the other hand tends to be less frequently heard, yet this word incorporates the most important aspect of budgeting. It means looking at situations in advance, thinking about the impact and implications of things in advance, and attempting to take control of situations in advance.

From the definition of budgets we distinguish three key components. First, we recognize the planning aspect of budget. The plan is regarded as the statement of intent or goal of the organization. The second aspect is the measurability. This makes it possible to measure the plan. The third component is time. It gives the possibility to say if the plan is achieved.

In summary, a budget is a statement setting out the monetary, numerical or non-quantitative aspects of an organization's plans for the coming week, month or year. Budgetary control is the analysis of what happened when those plans came to be put into practice, and what the organization did or did not do to correct for any variations from these plans.

CHARACTERISTICS OF A BUDGET

Gregory (2005) gives characteristics of a good budget. According to him, a good budget is characterizes by the following:

a. Participation – involves many people as possible in drawing up a budget,

b. Comprehensiveness- embraces the whole organization;

c. Standards – based it on established standards of performance;

d. Flexibility – allows for changing circumstances;

e. Feedback – constantly monitor performance;

f. Analysis of costs and revenues – this can be done on the basis of product line, departments or cost enters.

TYPES OF BUDGET

Gregory (ibid) identifies two main types of budget. These are traditional budget and MTEF budget. The traditional budget is a tool used by money experts to get your financial situation on track. Examples of the traditional budget are the following:

Fixed budget

Fixed budgets are often used by firms which rely on their forecasts. Hofstede (1968) writes that one discussed issue in the accounting literature is whether a budget should be fixed or variable with respect to volume or sales or other inputs. The fixed budget is therefore a budget which once made and accepted cannot be changed for whatever reason being that fixed cost are incurred and still persists irrespective of sales volume.

Flexible Budget

In the view of Garrison (2000), a flexible budget reflects the effect of changes in the budgeting environment which affect the performance of the budget, it does not confine itself to only one level of activity and actual results do not have to be compared against budgeted costs at the original activity level.

Capital Budget

Pandy (1999) defines capital budgeting as the firm's decision to invest an entity's current funds most efficiently in long-term activities in anticipation of an expected flow of the future benefits over a series of years.

Sales Budget

Stanton (1971) mentions that the cornerstone of successful marketing plan in a firm is the measurement and forecasting of market demand. The key figure needed is the sales forecasts because it is the basis for all budgeting and all operation in the firm. Radford and Richardson (1963) expressed their view that "effectiveness of budgetary control depends on the accuracy of sales estimates." In profit making organizations, the sales budget is very important because it helps in determining profit for the year.

The Medium-Term Expenditure Framework (MTEF)

Gregory (ibid) mentions that a medium-term expenditure framework budget consists of a top-down estimates of aggregate resources available for public expenditure consistent with macro-economic stability; bottom-up estimate of the cost of carrying out policies, both existing and new; and a frame work that reconcile these cost with aggregate resources.

The MTEF budget is a rolling process repeated every year and aims at reducing the imbalances between what is affordable and what is demanded by line ministries. MTEF does this by bringing together policy-making, planning, and budgeting early in the budgeting cycle, with adjustments taking place through policy changes. It involves building domestic macro-economic and sector modeling capacity. Also, even if the whole of the Government's budgeting system is working well, each sector is better if managing itself with a medium-term perspective.

A well implemented MTEF budget should:
1. Link the Government's priorities with a budget within a sustainable spending envelope;
2. Highlight the tradeoffs between the competing objectives of the Government;
3. Links budgets with the policy choices made;
4. Improve outcomes by increasing transparency, accountability, and the predictability of funding.

The MTEF budget was introduced in Ghana in 1999. It is a three year rolling expenditure program with the first tranche covering 1999-2001 to be continued thereafter. The second phase of the program was arranged to cover the preparation of composite budgets that is in line with sectorial policy objectives of regional activities, administration and district assemblies. Source: Ghana Government Budget Statement, 1992.

Adams et al (2003), identifies five different classes of budget; activity based budgeting, Zero-based, value based, profit planning and rolling budget and forecast.
1. Activity Based Budgeting (ABB), Activity based budgeting (ABB) is similar to activity based costing (ABC) and activity based management (ABM). ABB actually involves planning and controlling along the lines of value adding activities and processes. Resource and capital allocations decisions are consistent with ABM analysis, which involves structuring the organization's activities and business processes so that they better meet costumers and external need. From the perspective of Wilhelmi and Kleiner (1995), ABB can be applied in all industries and in all functions, including service industries and overhead functions. It also can be used in manufacturing. It is really a management

process, operating at the activity level, for continuous improvement on performance and costs.

2. Zero-Based Budgeting

The Zero based budgeting (ZBB), expenditures must be re-justified during each budgeting cycle rather than basing budgets on previous years or periods. ZBB is not build on inefficiencies and inaccuracies of previous history. The author also noted that the value of this approach depends on the stability of operating environment.

3. Value-Based Budgeting

This is a formal and systematic approach for managing the creation of shareholders value over time. All expenditure plans are evaluated as project appraisals and assessed in terms of the shareholder value they will create. This helps to link strategy and shareholder value to planning and budgeting.

4. Profit Planning Budgeting

This is about planning the future financial cash flows of profit centers (profit wheel), it gives the possibility to assess whether an organization or unit generates sufficient cash flows, creates economic value and attracts sufficient financial resources for investment. It also ensures consideration of an organization's short and long term prospects when preparing its financial plans.

5. Rolling Budgets and Forecast

6. It appears to have the most potential as the better regular budgeting approach. It enables firms improve their forecast accuracy and overcome the traditional budgeting time lag problem

This is by: solving the problems associated with frequent budgeting, being more responsive to changing circumstances, but requiring permanent resource to administer, and overcome problems linked to budgeting to a fixed point in time – i.e. the year end and the often dubious practices such cut-offs encouraged. Oduro (2001) on his part outlines budget types in the public sector as follows:

a. Line-item budget
b. Performance budget
c. Incremental budget
d. Zero based budget
e. Planning program budgetary system (PPBS)

Line Item Budget

This is a type of budget where expenditure is expressed considerable details with less attention being paid to the activities to be undertaken. The object of expenditure is the key to classification. This may also be called an 'indicative budget' if it is in a preliminary stage (pre-approval stage). It shows the nature of spending rather than its purpose

Performance Budget

This is a budgeting system which classifies items according to direct output of activity, intermediate products, activities, and purpose. It focuses on output or outcome rather than input and it is characterized by expenditure by work load or unit cost of activity, primary futures tasks and activities orientation management.

Incremental Budget

This is where the current budget is increased to allow for expected future conditions.

Resources are allowed based on what was received in previous years rather than on any rational allocation based on the policy and planning process. Any changes in priority are accommodated at the margin rather than through a revision to the allocation of the available financial resources. This approach entails the use of the previous year's budget as a baseline and adds or subtracts amounts to form that budget to reflect assumption for the forthcoming budget year.

BUDGET FORMULATION AND IMPLEMENTATION

In Ghana each MMDA by law has a budget unit, which has the responsibility of liaising with the District Coordinating Director (DCD), the District Finance Officer (DFO) and with the District Heads of Department to collate and prepare the draft budget.

The draft budget is thoroughly discussed by the Finance and Administration Sub Committee of the District Assembly. It is then submitted to the General Assembly through the Executive Committee of the Assembly for debate and approval.

In December each year, the Assembly sits and considers the draft budget and subjects it to thorough debate. Like Parliament, the Assembly debates on the budget and the debate could be very intense and critical, subject to detail analysis of revenue and expenditure as well as proposal for development plans. The current practice is that the Finance and Administration

Sub-Committee (F&A) of the Assembly and the related Units of District Co-coordinating

Directorate prepare their revenue and expenditure projections and classify them as the budget of the District Assembly.

At the last quarter of each year, AEDA like all other Assemblies, submit yearly budgets to the Regional Co-coordinating Council (RCC) in Greater Accra detailing the revenue and expenditure of the district for the ensuing year. The RCC collates and co-ordinates the budget of their respective MMDAs in the regions into a regional budget and submits them to the Ministry of Finance and Economic Planning. Copies are also sent to the National Development Planning Commission (NDPCU) for national planning purposes. There are instances that draft budgets are rejected by the Assembly calling for changes in certain aspects of the proposal submitted. A resolution of an Assembly is passed to approve the budget for the ensuing year after the debate and necessary changes. Source: AEDA Planning Unit

The implementation of the budget after the formulation stage involves;

1. Allocating responsibilities and resources;
2. Monitoring and evaluating performance;
3. Collecting and analyzing financial and non-financial data to determine variances and deviations;
4. Reaching a conclusion after comparing all the alternative choices made;
5. Taking corrective and comprehensive measures or actions to overcome the variances and deviation.

PREPARATION OF BUDGET AND BUDGETARY CONTROLS

Maitland (2001) mentions that the process of preparing and agreeing on a budget is a means of translating the overall objectives of the organization into detailed, feasible plan of action.

Public budget preparation is one of the tedious tasks that any country should look upon. The preparation process for the annual budget involves a great deal of energy, time, and expense. Hence, it is important that a country must be able to follow accurately all the methods of preparing an annual budget. In budgeting, the focus is not only to prepare the budget, but more importantly to have a follow-up operation for budgeting and to act according to known data. Based on this, Falk (1994) states that budgets are financial expressions of a country's plan for a period of time. It tells where and how the organization will spend money and where the money will come from to pay these expenses. He adds that budgets set limits. He says, "Imagine how chaotic an industry or country would be if everyone was allowed to spend as much as they wished on whatever they wanted." Besides setting limits, Andrews and Hill (2003) say that budgets also provides the assurance that the most important needs of a country are met first and less important needs are deferred until there are sufficient funds in which to pay for them. Even though budget preparation is not the sole thing that needs consideration in budgeting, the basis of it is still needed in order to have at least close estimation.

The Budget Cycle

In both the private and public sectors, the budget is prepared by the budget committee having regard to the organization's objectives. In a company, it is submitted to the board of directors or chief executive for approval. When approved it becomes an executive order. At the national level, the national budget is approved by both Cabinet and the Legislature before it becomes operational. It would be easy to dismiss the budgeting process as beginning when the first budget is prepared, and as being complete when the master budget is finalized. In reality, the budgeting process begins for many organizations a long time before the budget period begins and the process ends once the budget period has ended. This means that budgeting process is a very lengthy process. Typically, for a large organization, the pre-budgeting phase can begin up to a year before the budget period starts Adu-Gyamfi (2008). Jones and Pendlebury (1984) give some insight into the beginning of the budgeting cycle when they present a time table for preparation of detailed revenue budget and capital program for a local authority. They show that the process starts in June in the year preceding the budget period with the draft budget manual being sent to Finance Officers, who will discuss this draft with their departmental staff with a view to adoption or amendment. The budgetary planning phase is completed in March and made ready for an April discussion when the printed budget book is published and the approved estimates are put into the financial control system.

The Budget Period

The budget period is the period for which a set of budgets is prepared. Typically, according to Jones and Pendlebury (1984) the budget period is of one year's duration, and will be designed to coincide with an organization's or government's financial, or fiscal year. There is no reason why a budget period has to be one year, but typically it is made so.

These authorities on the other hand, say that if we are dealing with a project, then the budget will clearly be linked to that project. A three month project will have a budget covering the whole project and will thus be a three months budget. Most organizations will divide their budget period into calendar months or periods whereas others have thirteen period years all of an equal four week period.   In certain situations, the budget period will be analyzed according to some particular feature of the work in that situation. For example, stockbrokers have their year divided into "accounts" of two and three weeks' duration.   Indeed, these divisions of a budget period are control periods. In Ghana before 1999, government budget was prepared on yearly basis but with the introduction of the medium term expenditure frame work (MTFF), budget is prepared based on a three year rolling plan.

Finney (1994) outlines the following steps or cycle in preparing an effective budget:

1. Budget form and instructions are distributed to managers;
2. The form are filled out and submitted;
3. Individual budgets are transformed to appropriate budget and accounting terms and consolidated into an overall organizational budget;
4. The budget is reviewed, modified as necessary and approved;
5. The final budget is then used throughout the year to control and measure the organization.

Purposes of Budget Preparation

In the view of Williamson (1996) budgets should be prepared to serve the following purposes:

1. Planning

There is the likelihood that managers may be tempted not to plan for future operations because of day to day pressures and operating challenges. The budgeting planning process ensures that managers do plan for future operations and that they consider how conditions in the next year might change and what steps they should take now to respond to these changed conditions.

2. Coordination

This brings different parts of the budget together, reconciled into a common plan. Budgets are not prepared for the benefit of individuals involved in the process but for the best interest of the business or the stakeholders. Without guidance therefore, managers might make their own decision that will work against the overall objective of the business.

3. Communication

Everyone in the budget preparation chain must be aware of their input to the success of the entity's financial plan. This will ensure that all are made accountable for the implementation of the budget. This will also help in coordinating all budget activities for smooth implementation of the plan.

4. Motivation

The budget provides a standard which managers will evaluate their performance with. If they meet their targets regularly, they may be motivated to go for a higher target. If budget are dictated from above and imposed on those who are to implement the plan, it will rather not motivate workers and may be resisted. It can also serve as a useful device for influencing management behavior and motivating managers to perform in line with the organizational objectives.

5. Control

Planned activities can be compared to the actual so that effort will be concentrated on ascertaining the reasons behind the differences.   By investigating the reasons for the differences, managers may be able to identify inefficiencies such as the purchases of inferior quality materials. Appropriate control action will then be taken when reasons for inefficiencies have been found.

6. Performance Evaluation

As a manager you will like to evaluate your own performance even if you are not assessed by your superior. However performance is often evaluated by measuring a manager's performance against budget and the ability to achieve the targets would lead to promotion or bonus. The budget thus provides a very useful means of informing managers of how well they are performing in meeting targets that they have previously helped to set.

Williamson (Ibid) shares the view that, budgets are simply exercises in calculation unless they are used. When an organization draws a budget it does so as part of a system of budgetary control. The controls are some basic ideas of what the entity wants to do. It prepares budgets to help to achieve those ideas; and then once that is done whatever it is that has to be done, budgetary controls check to see if expenditures are on course.

2.3.4 Budgetary Controls

Budgetary Control is define by the Chartered Institute of Management Accountants (CIMA) (2007) as the establishment of mechanism authorizing responsibilities of executives to the requirements of a policy and the continuous comparison of actual with budgeted results either to secure by individual action the objective of a policy or to provide a basis for its revision. Hoftsede (1998) defines budgetary controls as planning translated into monetary terms. At the beginning, a budget is a plan and at the end it is a control device for measurement. In the view of Slim (1994) budgetary Controls aims at providing a formal basis for monitoring the progress of the organization as a whole and of its component parts towards the achievement of the objectives specified in the budget. Budgetary controls predetermine plans or standards of output and estimated incomes are compared with actual results and necessary corrective action taken.

Otley (1990) mentions that budgetary control is the main integrative control method for most business enterprises and the organization's business plan can be represented financially by the budget. The budget can thus be used as a monitor and control method for the complex issues of the business plan. Lucey (Ibid) argues that no system of planning can be successful without having an effective and efficient system of control. Budgeting is closely connected with control. The exercise of control in the organization with the help of the budget is known as budgetary control.

The process of budgetary control includes:
a. Preparation of various budgets;
b. Continuous comparison of actual performance with budgetary performance;
c. Revision of budgets in the light of changed circumstances.

The design of budgetary control system is dependent on several factors. These factors determine how easy to exercise controls in an organization. Hoftsede G.H (Ibid) argues that budgetary controls are easiest in organizations where:
a. The objectives are clear and unambiguous;
b. Outputs are measurable;
c. The effects of interventions are known;
d. The activities are repetitive.
e. Hoftsede (ibid) identifies six types of control which are suited to different situations:

1. Routine control can be used where all the four conditions above exist;
2. Expert control is needed when the activity is not repetitive but all other conditions are met;
3. Trial and error controls are used when the effect of intervention is not known but all other conditions are met. In budgeting, flexible budgeting and sensitivity analysis are examples of trial and error controls;
4. Intuitive control has to be used where an activity is not repetitive and the effects of interventions are not known. Budgeting for an investment in a project where the market is uncertain is an example of intuitive control;
5. Judgmental control is required when the objectives are clear but the outputs are not easily measurable;
6. Political control which is applicable where none of the Hofstede's conditions for easy control applies. Political control uses power structures, rules and rituals for the manipulation of scarce resources and negotiation processes. It can be seen in public sector organizations such as ministries, Departments and Agencies (MMDAs) where different Departments are all seeking to meet different objectives, resources are limited and there is high degree of bureaucracy.

Budgetary control in this case enable political control take place by providing an opportunity for negotiation and aiding manipulation and control of scarce resources.

Drury (2006) opines that two main budgetary controls exist. These are feed forward and feedback control. The feed forward control comes into being when the predictions are matched against desired outcomes. The purpose of feed forward control system is to anticipate errors or variances before they happen and to take steps to minimize them. The feedback control system is the measure of differences between planned and actual results so that subsequent actions can be modified to achieve the required results. He goes further to say that, the master budget is the budgeted profit and loss and balance sheet for the coming period which will be used as a basis for decision-making and control.

Budgetary control systems are so dependent on internal and external factors which affect the organization and changes in those factors must have impact on the budget. External, political, social and economic changes tend to have a slow effect on organizations as such changes are often unpredictable and organizations tend to act reactively rather than proactively. For example in the public sector, changes in the vision of a government from vision 2020 to vision 2015 will have an impact on their budget. Also economic changes such as the rate of inflation will affect the predictive value of budgets. If these changes occur frequently then organizations will increasingly need to use techniques such as flexible budgeting and sensitivity analysis to the effect of these changes.

Lowe et al (2002) say that while there appears to be general agreement of the behavioral, planning and control or objectives of budget control, its implementation can be problematic.

To understand the reason for this, one does not look inside the organization but also at the outside environment and the unpredictable of that context. In both private and public sectors, accountability is being driven down the organization to the level of the individual. Problems of budget control is how to control in an environment where there are also changing patterns both inside and outside the organizations.

Ashford (1989) posits that budgeting can be applied to virtually every situation. It does not matter whether we work in the public or privates sector of the economy. We may work for a profit making business or a non-profit making business. A company may be engaged in trading, manufacturing, or providing a service. In all of these situations, budgeting and budgetary control is utmost importance.

Adu –Gyamfi (2008) notes that budgetary controls can be achieved in MMDAs through many ways including the establishment of the following:

1. Budget committee;
2. Project committee
3. Investment committee;

Budgetary controls are also achieved through enforcement of internal controls in the form of:

a. Internal audits;
b. Internal checks within functions and activities;
c. Administrative controls in terms of ensuring effective personnel policies, operational rules, regulation, procedures and methods;
d. Segregation of duties into initiation, approval, authorizations, execution and recording of transactions;
e. Chart of accounts which indicate cost items, cost centers, cost levels and expenditure boundaries;
f. Maintenance of proper books of accounts which are books of prime entry, cash book, journals and ledgers;
g. g. Issuing accounting instructions in respect of purchase, stock and receipts, periodic stock-taking and imprest retirement and reimbursements;
h. Issue of accounting manuals and adoption of accounting policies in respect of assets disposals and depreciation.

In achieving effective budgetary controls, the Audit Service Law, Act 654 (2004) makes it mandatory for public sector entities to establish Audit Report Implementation Committees (ARICs).

ARICs are not only to examine audit reports but also evaluate budgetary control systems in MDAs and MMDAs. Audits of financial transactions and the final accounts periodically at least annually and the issuing of audit reports timely cannot be over – emphasized in budgetary controls.

However, this is something which is usually lacking with public accounts. Preparation of government accounts sometimes delays leading to weak accountability and transparency in the MMDAs as well as the central government machinery.

Financial statements of the government are useful for external control purposes and are subject to external verifications by tax payers, donors, investors, suppliers, bankers and constituents.

They help key stakeholders to make informed financial decisions.

The use of budget as tool for control measures by Ghanaian local authorities is certainly not just of recent date. Governments have always used budget and budget control measures to plan and control public projects and programs. In the view of Amoako and Acquah (2008), early local government organizations were established to ensure some level of collective protection against the human and natural disasters were not of course comparable with our modern MMDAs. Amoako and Acquah (2008) conceptualize that, for MMDAs to be effective, their budgets must be aligned with their strategies, strategic management and performance. This is supported by Blumetritt (2006), who says there is the need for organizations to integrate their strategic management with their annual budgets.

Budgets and budget control measures are used as a tool for various reasons such as:

i. To set the objective of governmental organizations;

ii. To achieve measurable results;

iii. To measure operational processes;

iv. To achieve accountability.

The control over the budget is also related on the management of which comes in different type of controls. In assuring that the funds are clearly budgeted, the managers' conduct auditing procedures and financial reporting to observe if there is any evidence of its misuse or to seek the call for additional budgetary allowance.

Havens (2000) points that different risk and assumptions can be established if there was no internal control on the financial transactions of a business. Resources can be wasted, fraud, inaccurate and erroneous accounting may occur, projects completion could be inefficient coupled with failure to produce timely and reliable financial and management information.

All of these risks will lead to the downfall of the organization. Budgetary controls, according to Larson and Madson (1999) are implemented in the public sector to aid management activities of the company's public funds.

THE BUDGET AS A TOOL FOR MEASURING FINANCIAL PERFORMANCE

Merchants and Stede (2003) postulate that performance relates to qualitative and quantitative description of results which can help shape the fortunes of an organization. The relevance of performance measurement is highlighted by the popular dictum "what you measure is what you get" (Kaplan and Norton, 1996). Bogt (2004) mentions that measurement relates to organizational activities, production or output and in the public sector performance measurement relates to primary activities and outcome resulting from public policy.

Performance measurement is simply a method for assessing progress towards stated goals. It is not intended to act as a reward or punishment mechanism, but rather as a communication and management tool. The goal of instituting performance measurement in government is to shift the focus from the amount of resources allocated, to the results achieved with those resources. Performance measurement in the public sector can serve a variety of purposes.

First, it serves as a vehicle for communication to the public, they signal the things that government deems important and how the government should be judged.

Second, it serves as a motivational tool to those within the organization, measures; signal what is important, and what is necessary for success. Finally, measures can serve as a vital management and decision-making tool, providing information that can be used to make improvements in program design and service delivery. (Alberta's Treasury Guide on Performance Measurement, 1996)

REASONS FOR MEASURING FINANCIAL PERFORMANCE

a. Behn (2003) gives eight reasons for adapting performance measurement in evaluating financial performance:

1. To evaluate how well a public agency is performing;
2. To enable public managers to ensure their subordinates are doing the right thing;
3. To budget – budgets are crude tools in improving performance;
4. To motivate for better results;
5. To enable organizations communicate their accomplishments to stakeholders especially owners;
6. To promote to convince citizens that an organization is doing well;
7. To learn;
8. To improve on current states.

In the view of Kaplan and Norton (Ibid), a general conception of the use of performance measurement is that, it is used to support the formulation and implementation of organizational strategy. This use of performance measures by Ghanaian MMDAs appears to be wide spread and pronounced nowadays. Budget and budgetary control measures are being used for both external oriented communications as well as for internal oriented strategic, political and operational reasons Bogt (2004).

Thompson (2007) states that, budgeting, strategies and strategic management share an orientation toward improving business performance, as each is used to set an organization on an appropriate path to success and guide its manager's decisions and activities.

Reginald L et al (1971) look at budget as the system and process that integrates all the operational plans to express the financial results and economic performance of a business and that the total financial consequences resulting from some of all operating plans is the final measure of economic performance.

Managerial performance is often evaluated by the extent to which budgetary target for which individual managers are responsible have been achieved. Managerial rewards such as bonuses or performance-related pay can also be linked to achievement of budgetary targets. Managers can also use the budget to evaluate their own performance and clarify how close they are to meet agreed performance targets. In this sense, budgeting serves as a measuring rod.

BENEFITS OF A BUDGET

Lucey (ibid) outlines the benefits of budget as follows:

a. It provides clear guidelines for managers and supervisions and is the major way which organizational objectives are translated into specific tasks and objectives related to individual managers;
b. The budgetary process is an important method of communication and coordination both vertically and horizontally;
c. Because of the exception principle, which is at the heart of budgetary control, management time can be saved and attention directed to areas of most concern;
d. The integration of budgets makes possible better cash and working capital management;
e. Better control of current operations is helped by regular, systematic monitoring and reporting of activities;

f. Provided there is proper participation, goal congruence is encouraged and motivation increased. Kaplan (1992) also says that budget brings about improvement and efficiency in the working conditions of the organization by setting out target of the organization and providing resources to work towards achieving these targets thus everybody knows what they are working for and given the necessary resources which will ensure efficiency.

CHALLENGES OF A BUDGET

Lucey (ibid), identifies these as the challenges of a budget;
a. Variances frequent due to changing circumstances and poor forecasting due to managerial performance.
b. b. Budgets are developed round existing organization structures which may be inappropriate for current conditions.
c. The existence of well documented plans may cause inertia and lack of flexibility in adapting to change. Badly handled budgetary systems with undue pressure or lack of regard to behavioural factors may cause antagonism and may lower morale.

Drury (Ibid) opines that, budget could be seen as a pressure device imposed by management resulting in poor labour relations and inaccurate record keeping. Departmental conflicts over resource allocation and blaming each other when targets are not meet. It also involves a lot of guess work.

Adams et al (2003) explained the weakness of budgetary practices under several headings;

Competitive strategy:
Budgets are rarely strategically focused and are often contradictory; because
(a) They concentrate on cost reduction and not on value creation;
(b) They act as constrain to responsiveness and flexibility, and is often a barrier to change;
(c) They add little value, rather they turn to be bureaucratic and discourage creative thinking;
(d) They are time consuming and costly to put together;
(e) They are developed and updated too infrequently – usually annually;
(f) They are based on unsupported assumptions and guesswork; therefore encouraging gaming and perverse or dysfunctional behavior;
(g) They strengthen vertical command and control;
(h) They do not reflect the emerging network structures that organizations are adopting;
(i) They reinforce departmental barriers rather than encourage knowledge sharing; and
(j) They make people feel undervalued.

What Adams et al (ibid) are stressing is the fact that traditional planning and budgeting processes used in organizations are failing to deliver results. They are too time consuming to undertake, encourage internal politics and gaming behavior, and are too inward looking, with short-term culture that focuses on achieving a budget figure. They further say that budget as a management tool by itself is neither good nor bad. How managers administer budgets is the key to their value. When administered wisely, it facilitates planning and resource allocation and help to enumerate, itemize, dissect and examine all the products and services that the company offers to customers.

CRITERIA FOR MEASURING BUDGET PERFORMANCE

Selecting which measure to use is part art and part science. The choice of measures will largely depend upon the intended:

1. Understandability — the measure and information are clear and easily understood by the public, and sufficiently explain how performance is being assessed;
2. Relevance — the measure is an accurate representation of what is being measured. The information presented is timely and directly related to the subject matter;
3. Reliability — the information is free from error, unbiased and complete. Also, the results can be duplicated by others using the same information and methodology;
4. Comparability — results can be compared to other years or to similar organizations audience and what they want to know. (Alberta's Treasury Guideon Performance Measurement, 1996).

The primary focus of the government's performance measures is for public reporting purposes. Therefore, the foremost consideration is that the measures and the information they provide should be clear and easy to understand.

In measuring these budget performances, it is important for the manager to ask series of questions such as these:

1. Do the measures relate to the stated core businesses and goals?
2. Does the measure make sense and is the wording understandable?
3. Does the measure really indicate the effects government intends the program to have?
4. Is the outcome measured at least partially within the organization's ability to influence?
5. Can the measure show the extent to which goals have been achieved?
6. 6. Is the data accurate and can the information be collected over time on a consistent basis?
7. Has the data been impartially gathered and analyzed? Will the measures be valid for more than one period without significant changes?
8. Do the measures allow for comparisons with past performance and with other organizations?
9. Can others using the same data arrive at similar results or conclusions?
10. Is the cost of collecting the information reasonable?
11. Do the measures provide performance information on ministry/government priorities? (Alberta's Treasury Guide on Performance Measurement, 1996)

RESEARCH METHODOLOGY

A research such as this requires an organized data gathering in order to pinpoint the research philosophies and theories that will be included in the research, the methodology of the research and the instruments of the data interpretation. This chapter presents the profile of the study area and methodology adopted for data collection and analysis.

PROFILE OF ADA EAST DISTRICT ASSEMBLY (AEDA)

The Ada East District Assembly has been mandated by the Local Government Legal Instrument (L.I.1491) to champion the development of its jurisdiction in the year 1989. The Decentralization policy of Ghana has stimulated commitment towards the mobilization of local resources to improve rural lives. Key amongst such interventions is the realization of potential resources and other social externalities beyond the boundaries of every jurisdiction. Such resources, if identified, are to be fully exploited to manage the welfare of the people in that area and to subsequently work towards their betterment.

Location and Size

The Ada East District formally known as Dangme East District is situated in the Eastern part of the Greater Accra Region. It can be located between latitudes 5°45'S and 6°00'N and Longitude 0°20'W and 0°35'E. The total land area of the District is about <u>909 square km</u>, which represents almost 28% of the total land size of the Greater Accra Region. The District shares common boundaries with the North Tongu District to the North, South Tongu District and Dangme West District to the East and West respectively. It is bounded to the south by the Gulf of Guinea, which stretches over 45 kilometers (27.9 miles) from Kewunor to Wokumagbe. It is also bounded by the Volta River South–Eastwards extending to the Gulf of Guinea southwards thereby forming an Estuary, about 2 kilometers away from the District capital, Ada-Foah.

Topography

The District forms the central portions of the Accra plains. The relief is generally gently and undulating, a low plain with heights not exceeding 60 meters (200 ft) above sea level. The prominent relief features include the Tojeh boulders rising about 240 meters (800 ft) above sea level. These boulders are scattered irregularly over the sea. The photograph below portrays a devastated road from Ada-Foah-Otrokpe by tidal waves.

Drainage

The general drainage pattern of the Dangme East District can be described as dendritic with some of the streams taking their sources from the Volta River. Water bodies such as Anyamam, Akplabanya, Sege, and Tamatoku among others are sprung ups with increased and decreased capacities in the in wet and dry seasons respectively.

Vegetation

The vegetation is basically the coastal savannah type, characterized by short savannah grasses and interspersed with shrubs and short trees. Along the coast, there are stretches of coconut trees and patches of coconut groves which combine to give the area a classic look. A few strands of mangrove trees such as the Angor mangrove can also be found around the Songhor Lagoon and the tributaries of the Volta River where the soil is waterlogged and salty.

Climatic Conditions

The Ada East District is encapsulated by the south-eastern coastal plains of Ghana which is one of the hottest parts of the country. Temperatures are high throughout the year and ranges between 23°C and 28°C. A maximum temperature of 33°C is normally attainable during the very hot seasons. Rainfall is generally heavy during the major seasons between March and September. The average rainfall is about 750 millimeters. The area is however very dry during the harmattan season when there is no rainfall at all. Humidity is about 60 per cent high, due to the proximity of the sea, the Volta River and other water bodies. Daily evaporation rates range from 5.4 - 6.8 millimeters. The relatively high temperatures help in the quick crystallization of salt for the salt industry.

Revenue Sources

The main sources of revenue at AEDA are the IGF and Central Government transfers. The IGF is the primary source of revenue which is made up of fees and fines, rates, rents on lands, licenses and investments. The IGF is mainly used for recurrent expenditure such as; salaries and wages, Assembly member's allowances, utilities, maintenance and repairs and miscellaneous expenses. The central government transfers are revenues which are transferred from the central government sources to the MMDAs. These are DACF, Grants- in aid- DDF and Ceded revenue. Article 455 of the 1992 constitution which established the DACF defines the total revenue as all "revenues collected by or accruing to the Central government other than the foreign loans, grants, non-tax revenue and revenues already collected by or for District Assemblies under any enactment in force" The DACF is distributed among District Assemblies by a formula approved by parliament. Grants- in aid such as, District Development Fund or facility (DDF), Social Investment Fund (SIF), Community Water and Sanitation Project (CWSP),etc are given out by donors for specific projects Ceded revenues are transfers which the central governments tapped through the collection of taxes and ceded them to the District Assemblies in pursuit of decentralization.

Tables: Three Tables showing revenue and expenditure budgets of AEDA for the periods 2011, 2012, and 2013.

TABE 1: 2011

No	REVENUE HEAD	BUDGETED	ACTUALS	VARIENCES
		GH¢.00	GH¢.00	GH¢.00
1	RATE	82,007.00	46,464.40	35,542.60
2	DONOR GRANTS AND RELIEFS			0.00
3	NON GOVERNMENTAL AGENCIES			0.00
6	GRANTS –DISTRICTS DEVPMT FUND	3,701,961.12	2,227,040.61	1,474,920.51
5	INTEREST & INVESTMENT INCOME	17,000.00	8,066.00	8,934.00
6	LANDS AND ROYALTIES	19,550.00	50,674.00	-31,124.00
7	RENT OF LANDS, BUILDINGS &HOUSES	18,330.00	9,578.00	8,752.00
8	LICENCES	148,755.00	48,241.50	100,513.50
9	FEES &FINES	241,535.00	661,598.66	-420,063.66
10	FINES, PENALTIES &FORFEITS			0.00
11	MISCELLANEOUS &UNIDENTIFIED REVENUE	32,235.00	40,736.19	-8,501.19
A	**TOTAL REVENUE**	**4,261,373.12**	**3,092,399.36**	**1,168,973.76**
	EXPENDITURE HEAD			
1	COMPENSATION OF EMPLOYEES	492,332.62	189,653.28	302,679.34
2	TRAVELLIND &TRANSPORT	106,900.00	209,412.21	-102,512.21
3	CONSUMPTION OF FIXED CAPITAL			0.00
4	MAINTAINANCE, REPAIRS & RENEWALS	29240	67752.08	-38,512.08
5	CAPITAL EXPENDITURE	3302415.49	2,301,955.03	1,000,460.46
6	SOCIAL BENEFITS			0.00
7	OTHER EXPENSES	156,900.00	209,412.21	-52,512.21
B	**TOTAL EXPENDITURE**	**4,087,788.11**	**2,978,184.81**	**1,109,603.30**

TABE 2: 2012

No	REVENUE HEAD	BUDGETED	ACTUALS	VARIENCES
		GH¢.00	GH¢.00	GH¢.00
1	RATE	81,625.00	9,657.24	71,967.76
2	DONOR GRANTS AND RELIEFS	1,634,839.00	420,168.74	1,214,670.26
3	NON GOVERNMENTAL AGENCIES	2,180.00	0.00	
	GRANTS -DISTRICTS	6,789,903.32	1,930,590.15	4,859,313.17
4	INTEREST	0.00	0.00	0.00
6	LANDS AND ROYALTIES	40,530.00	54,995.00	-14,465.00
7	RENT OF LANDS, BUILDINGS &HOUSES	22,476.00	8,761.00	13,715.00
8	LICENCES		471,615.60	-471,615.60
9	FEES	124,310.00	56,979.07	67,330.93
10	FINES, PENALTIES &FORFEITS	5,500.00	3,863.80	1,636.20
11	MISCELLANEOUS &UNIDENTIFIED REVENUE	9,000.00	114,560.72	-105,560.72
A	TOTAL REVENUE	8,710,363.32	3,071,191.32	5,639,172.00
	EXPENDITURE HEAD			
1	COMPENSATION OF EMPLOYEES	1,170,747.82	135,032.20	1,035,715.62
2	USE OF GOODS OR SERVICE	769,714.14	541,771.45	227,942.69
3	CONSUMPTION OF FIXED CAPITAL			
4	INTEREST			
5	GRANTS		2,103,435.75	-2,103,435.75
6	SOCIAL BENEFITS	5,610,915.18	435	5,610,480.18
7	OTHER EXPENSES	11,059.00	52,281.87	-41,222.87
B	TOTAL EXPENDITURE	7,562,436.14	2,832,956.27	10,395,392.41

TABLE 3:   2013

No	REVENUE HEAD	BUDGETED	ACTUALS	VARIENCES
		GH¢.00	GH¢.00	GH¢.00
1	RATE	113,735.00	10,151.12	103,583.88
2	DONOR GRANTS AND RELIEFS	963,640.00	189,758.90	773,881.10
3	NON GOVERNMENTAL AGENCIES	1,000.00	0.00	1,000.00
4	GRANTS -DISTRICTS	5,763,569.00	1,270,294.91	4,493,274.09
5	INTEREST	0.00	0.00	0.00
6	LANDS AND ROYALTIES	52,000.00	42,947.00	9,053.00
7	RENT OF LANDS, BUILDINGS &HOUSES	31,200.00	14,798.00	16,402.00
8	LICENCES		114,098.90	114,098.90
9	FEES	135,645.30	67,750.29	67,895.01
10	FINES, PENALTIES &FORFEITS	7,580.00	2,603.00	4,977.00
11	MISCELLANEOUS &UNIDENTIFIED REVENUE	33,708.00	30,459.50	3,248.50
A	**TOTAL REVENUE**	**7,102,077.30**	**1,742,861.62**	**8,844,938.92**
	EXPENDITURE HEAD			
1	COMPENSATION OF EMPLOYEES	728,011.00	103,819.16	831,830.16
2	USE OF GOODS OR SERVICE	1,135,122.67	164,524.79	1,299,647.46
3	CONSUMPTION OF FIXED CAPITAL			
4	INTEREST			
5	GRANTS		850,577.84	
6	SOCIAL BENEFITS	5,683,459.33	1783.32	5,681,676.01
7	OTHER EXPENSES	9,559.32	17,826.00	-8,266.68
B	**TOTAL EXPENDITURE**	**7,556,152.32**	**1,138,531.11**	**5,673,409.33**

Source: AEDA 2011, 2012, 2013 financial statements.

The budget of the AEDA Assembly as shown on the table indicates a three year budget that is, 2011, 2012 and 2013. The budget is prepared based on the resources available to the Assembly. During these years the budgeted figures for revenue items are always higher than the actual revenue resulting in deficit whiles the actual figures for expenditures in general assessment are lower than the budgeted.

Table 4: A table showing development projects on-going by AEDA and their locations.

No	Project Title	Location	Name of Contractor	Contract Sum GH₵	Date of Award	Source of Funding	Expenditure to Date GH₵	% of Work done	Level of Completion
22	Const. of 1No. 6-Unit Clsrm Blk with ancillary facilities	Ada Foah - Presby School	El-Qud Enterprise Limited	146,990.91	12-Oct-10	GetFUND	48,148.00	76%	On-going
18	Const. of 1No. 6-Unit Clsrm Blk, Office & Store	Ada Technical Institute	J.D.D Company Limited	227,549.00	14-Jun-10	GetFUND		85%	On-going
20	Const. of 1No. 6-Unit Clsrm Blk & 2No. 3-Unit KVIP toilet	Amuyaok ope D/A Primary Sch.	Medium dwelling Com. Ltd	143,565.60	24-Sep-10	GetFUND		80%	On-going
21	Const. of 1No. 2-Storey, 12-Unit Clsrm Blk with ancillary facilities	Anyamam JHS	Nichuago Enterprise	251,431.62	12-Oct-10	GetFUND	71,083.80	40%	On-going
23	Const. of 1No. 6-Unit Clsrm Blk with	Aplabanya Primary School	Delovely Co. Limited	149,116.00	12-Oct-10	GetFUND	33,617.25	80%	On-going

	ancillary facilities								
	Completion of 1No. 2-Storey, 6-Unit Clsrm Blk with ancillary facilities	Big - Ada Methodist	Obifod Company Limited	262,299.40	6-Jun-11	GetFUND	47,720.00	70%	On-going
38	Const. of 1No. 3-Unit Clsrm Blk with ancillary facilities	Englisi Kenya D/A Primary	Nichuago Enterprise	149,640.65	28-Oct-11	GetFUND		20%	On-going
25	Const. of 1No. 6-Unit Clsrm Blk with ancillary facilities	Faithkope Primary School	Nu-Skin Limited	146,313.31	12-Oct-10	GetFUND	48,884.11	60%	On-going
39	Const. of 1No. 6-Unit Clsrm Blk with ancillary facilities	Luhuese D/A Primary	Nezerdo limited	195,525.86	28-Oct-11	GetFUND		30%	On-going
40	Const. of 1No. 6-Unit Clsrm Blk with ancillary facilities	Pute Presby Primary	Almighty Investment Limited	198,094.12	28-Oct-11	GetFUND		25%	On-going
26	Const. of 1No. 6-Unit	Sege - Sorkope Primary	Acod Const. Limited	145,703.47	19-Oct-10	GetFUND	19,361.07	65%	On-going

Clsrm Blk with ancillary facilities	School								
Const. of 1No. 6-Unit Clsrm Blk with ancillary facilities	Sege - Sorkope Primary School	Acod Const. Limited	145,703.47	19-Oct-10	GetFUND	19,361.07	65%	On-going
Const. of 1No. 6-Unit Clsrm Blk & 2No. 3-Unit KVIP toilet	Toflokpo Primary School	Josado Commercial Services	131,895.40	24-Sep-10	GetFUND		80%	On-going
Const. of 1No. 6-Unit Clsrm Blk with ancillary facilities	Toflokpo-Salom D/A Primary Sch.	Adomina Co. Limited	141,761.07	12-Oct-10	GetFUND	31,896.24	65%	On-going

Source: AEDA Works Department, May 2014

Table 5

FOURTH (4TH) QUARTER 2013 PROGRESS REPORT

NO	DESCRIPTION OF PROJECT	LOCATION	CONTRACTOR	CONTRACT SUM (GHC)	DATE OF AWARD	COMPLETION DATE	SOURCE OF FUNDING	EXPENDITURE TO DATE (GHC)	GENERAL REMARKS	
									% OF WORK DONE	LEVEL OF COMP.
1.	Construction of 1No. 8-	Otrokpe	Osfam Limited	51,270.00	25-Aug-11	25-Nov-11	DACF	51,270.00	100	Completed with retention paid

	Seater Water Closet Toilet	Comm unity								and yet to be handed over
2.	Construct ion of a Buyback Center	Tojeh Comm unity	Enarcu Const. Limited	307,64 9.63	4-Nov-11	04-Feb-12	LSDGP	198,24 1.21	71	Plasteri ng Stages
3.	Water Distributi on Extensio n to 9 Commun ities	Asigbe kope and Pute areas (attach ed)	El-Qud Enterpr ise Limited	155,03 9.26	8-Mar-11	6-June-11	LSDGP	125,79 6.13	85	Finishin g Stages
4.	Const. of 1No. 2-storey Tourist Center (Phase 1: Ground Floor)	Ada-Foah (Work s Dept.)	Enarcu Const. Limited	450,62 5.30	24-Feb-11	25-Sep-11	DDF	83,364 .86	45	Revised contract sum due to change in design
5.	Const. of 1no. 6 unit Clsrm block with ancillary facilities	Ada Foah Presby School	El-Qud Enterpr ise	146,99 0.91	12-Oct-10	12-Apr-11	GET Fund	68,757 .38	70	Plasteri ng Stages
6.	Const. of 1No. 6 Clsrm block with ancillary facilities	Faithk ope Primar y School	Nu-skin Limited	146,31 3.31	12-Oct-10	12-Apr-11	GET Fund	67,133 .44	70	Plasteri ng Stages
7.	Completi on of 1No. 2-storey, 6-Unit	Big-Ada Metho dist	Obifod Compa ny Limited	262,29 9.40	6-Jun-11	07-Feb-12	GET Fund	47,720 .00	90	Painting Stages

No.	Project	Community	Contractor	Contract Sum	Date Awarded	Completion Date	Source of Funding	Amount Paid	%	Remarks
	Clsrm Block with ancillary facilities	School								
8.	Const. of 1No. 3-Unit Clsrm Block with ancillary facilities	Englisi Kenya D/A Primary School	Nichuago Enterprise	149,640.65	28-Oct-11	06-Jul-12	GET Fund	75,666.75	80	Finishing Stages
9.	Const. of 1No. 6-Unit Clsrm Block with ancillary facilities	Luhuese D/A Primary	Nezerdo Limited	195,525.86	28-Oct-11	06-Jul-12	GET Fund	106,551.08	70	Plastering Stages
10.	Const. of 1No. 6-Unit Clsrm Block with ancillary facilities	Pute Presby Primary	Almighty Investment limited	238.094.12	28-Oct-11	06-Jul-12	GET Fund	-	60	Lintel level
11.	Const. of 1No. 6-Unit Clsrm Block for Ada Technical Institute	Atortorkope	J. D. D. Co. Limited	227,549.00	14-Jul-10	18-Oct-11	GET Fund	-	100	Completed and yet to be handed over
12.	Construction of 3-Storey Dist. Administration	Atortorkope	Bawa Huud Ltd.	793,610.88	11-Jun-07	14-June-08	DACF	712,510.00	70	Finishing Stages

	Block									
13.	Completion of Kindergarten Basic School at Ocanseykope	Ocanseykope	Danmuz Construction Company Ltd.	49,886.43	24-Oct-12	14-Dec-12	DACF	49,886.43	100	Completed with retention paid and yet to be handed over
14.	Construction of 2No. 4 units Nurses Quarters at Faithkope	Faithkope	Community Labour Work	202,000.00	15-Feb-12	14-April-12	GSOP	194,358.00	100	Completed and yet to be handed over
15.	Regravelling of Senakeykope-Teikpitikope-Gorm Feeder Road (4.60Km)	Senakeykope-Teikpitikope-Gorm	Evesafe Company Ltd.	145,576.20	22-Jan-13	21-May-13	GSOP	-	80	Compacting of graveled Road
16.	Planting of 40,000 seedlings at Two (2) communities (Dikanya & Peterkope)	Dikanya & Peterkope	Community Labour Work	40,000.00	19-Feb-12	19-Feb-13	GSOP	26,482.00	100	Seedlings has fully acclimatized at the 2 communities

Source: AEDA Planning Unit, May 2014

POPULATION AND SAMPLING TECHNIQUES

The population of the study consists of the entire management consisting of District Chief Executive (DCE), District Coordinating Director (DCD), Heads of Department (HODs) and staff of the Assembly and the various departments, it includes members of various sub-committees, Assembly Members including the Presiding Member, Budget Committee Members, Commissioned revenue collectors, traders, tax payers and Regional Budget Staff at RCC in Accra. The sample in the study was used to select fifty (50) respondents.

The study used non-scientific or judgment sampling to select the sample size and respondents.

Advantages in using the non-scientific or judgments sampling are the following;

1. The researcher had an opportunity to use his own intuition, experience and judgment in selecting the sample size and the respondents;
2. There was no need to use statistical or mathematical method which requires some mathematical or statistical calculations;
3. It allowed the researcher to consider social issues and circumstance in the random selection of the sample size, the respondents and drawing conclusions;
4. The technique avoided delays in the determination of the sample size and who should be a respondent;
5. It allowed the researcher to draw conclusions about the population which were quite representative.

Classification of Respondents and Sample size for the purpose of this research, respondents were classified as follows:

Category and Number

1. Political and Administrative Heads   3
2. Other HODs   5
3. Other Staff   10
4. Fin. & Adm. Sub-C'tee 5
5. Assembly Members including Presiding Member 5
6. Revenue Collectors 5
7. Accounts and Budget Staff of the Assembly 5
8. Tax / Rate   payers 12
   Total   50

DATA COLLECTION PROCEDURE

The research depended on primary and secondary sources for data collection. The primary sources of data came from interviews, questionnaires, discussions and observations. The primary data frequently provided the detailed data which were actual situations or responses arising out of the field study. The secondary sources of data were from published and unpublished articles, from social science journals, thesis as well as related studies on budgeting and accounting in MMDAs annual budget reports, monthly trial balances and financial statements.

DATA COLLECTION INSTRUMENTS

The data collection instruments were mainly questionnaires, interviews, observation and face-to-face discussions with key respondents. The questionnaires were in three parts, those questionnaires administered to key staff, other departmental staff and revenue and tax payers. In all seventy (70) questionnaires were sent to all respondents. Respondents were asked to answer the questions or give their views and opinions to the researcher. Fifty-five (55) questionnaires were returned. Ten (10) were not retrieved and Five (5) were rejected because respondents did not answer them the way they were expected. Fifty (50) questionnaires were considered quite well and accepted for use in the study. The questionnaires were administered for three weeks before they were collected.

RESEARCH DESIGN

This study considers research design which provides framework for collection of data and analysis of data an important element. The descriptive approach requires the use of observations in the study. The purpose of employing this method is to describe the budgeting system in MMDAs in general and AEDA in particular and to explore the causes of a budget variances. The researcher opted to use this kind of research method considering the desire to obtain first hand data from respondents so as to draw rational and sound conclusions and make recommendations for improvement in budgetary controls.

DATA ANALYSIS

Data collected were edited, evaluated and measured against the research to ensure their completeness, consistency, accuracy and relevance. Microsoft software was used in the processing of primary and secondary data gathered through the administration of the data collection instruments. This is to enable data gathered to be presented into tables, graphs and charts for qualitative explanations and analysis on budgeting and budgetary controls.

DATA PRESENTATION AND ANALYSIS

This chapter presents data which were gathered from the field through questionnaires administered, interviews conducted, observations, discussions, telephone conversations and face to face conversations with respondents in respect of budget preparation and budgetary controls which ensure prudent cash flows. Records, documents and other forms of information from the District Assembly and the Central government were also used to complement the primary data. Based upon these tables, graphs and charts are used to give true facts about budgeting and budgetary control processes in the Assembly.

ANALYSIS OF DATA

Seventy (70) questionnaires were sent to all respondents and respondents were asked to answer the questions or give their views and opinions to the researcher. A more than fair response rate was obtained as Fifty-five (55) questionnaires were completed and returned. It is worth noting that the Fifty-five (55) questionnaires received is a reflection of the fact that 79% percent of the respondents returned the questionnaires. Five (5) questionnaires were rejected because respondents did not answer them the way they were expected. Fifty (50) questionnaires were considered quite good and accepted for the research and Ten (10) were not retrieved.

Fifteen (15) respondents were randomly selected for face-to-face interviews. During the interviews the researcher listened attentively to what the respondents said, what they intended saying and what they had difficulty in saying due to their social, psychological or political indications. The researcher had discussion with District Chief Executive (DCE), District Coordinating Director (DCD), District Finance Officer (DFO), Budget Officer, three (3) Revenue Collectors, four(4) revenue and tax payers, members of the budget committee, chairman of the Finance and Administration Sub-Committee (F&A) of the Assembly on revenue collection, payment and management to get the true picture about budgets, budgetary controls and personal integrity. The researcher had occasions to ascertain the true budgeting procedures and examine budget actuals and forecasts between 2011, and 2014 to determine if there are possible variances.

ANALYSIS OF BIOGRAPHICAL INFORMATION OF RESPONDENTS

It was considered imperative that the biographical information of the respondents be presented to determine how such information influence responses given by respondents.

These data form a comprehensive picture of the quantity and quality of responses. The biographical information is presented in chart form in figure A (1), and A (2) below. The data are given according to departments and qualification.

The population of the study is composed of the management and staff of the Assembly and its decentralized departments. Findings as depicted in figure1 (A) indicate that 50% of the respondents are the management and staff of AEDA, 30% constitute other department staff and 20% are the non-staff respondents. It is encouraging to note that 48% of the respondents have Bachelor Degrees, which is an indication of the fact that greater number of the respondents is not ignorant about budgeting processes and budgetary controls.

Table 4 A shows distribution of the respondents.

RESPONDENTS	PER CENTAGES
Management and Staff of the Assembly	50%
Other Staff	30%
Non-Staff	20%
Total	100%

Source : Field data 20th May, 2014

Fig 1A CHART OF RESPONDENTS

Table 5 A shows Qualification of the respondents.

QUALIFICATION	PER CENTAGES
MASTERS	3%
CHARTERED ACCOUNTANT(ICA Gh)	2%
FIRST DEGREE	48%
HIGHER NATIONAL DEPLOMA (HND)	30%
OTHERS	17%

Source : Field data 20th May, 2014

Fig 2 A: QUALIFICATION OF RESPONDENTS

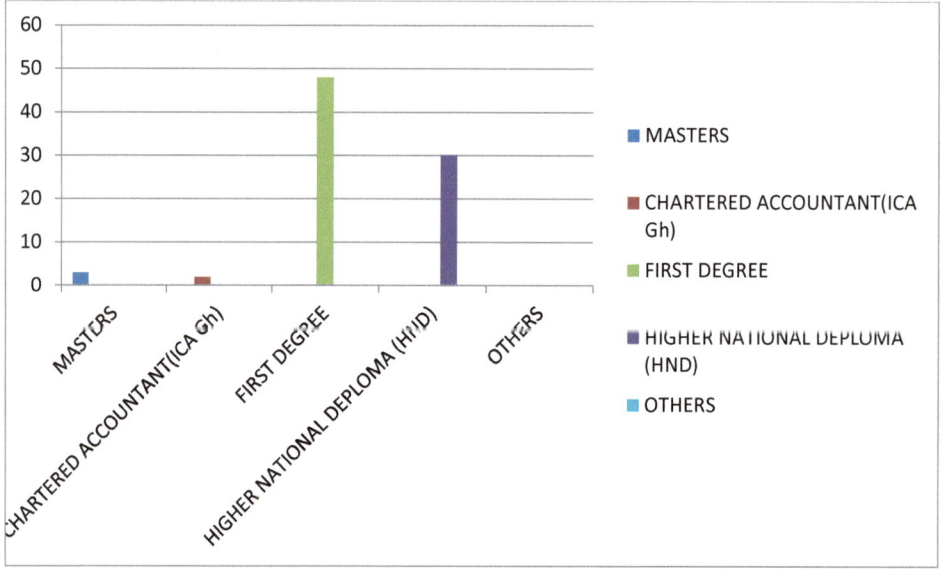

BUDGET PLANNING, PREPARATION AND IMPLEMENTATION

The research revealed that AEDA has a long range plan which covers a period of five (5) years. However, the long range plan is reviewed by the Assembly annually to make some changes where necessary. It was realized from all the respondents that AEDA has a budget committee which monitor the budget preparation, implementation and post implementation to ensure that actual performance conforms to the budgeted plans and seven (7) members are on the budget committee.

The budget committee requires that all heads of departments prepare and submit their proposals to the budget committee for discussion, review and approval. Departmental managers attend budget committee meeting to defend their proposals.

As to whether respondents know the budget processes, 70% answered in the affirmative and said various departments prepare their budget proposals and submit them to the budget committee for discussion, review and approval. Departmental managers then attend budget committee meetings to defend their estimates and proposals.

Respondents say their Departments prepare various types of budgets. 70% of the respondents were of the view that the cash budget for example is prepared to cater for cash inflows and outflows for the budget year. Labour budget is prepared to cater for remuneration of personnel whiles the capital budget is prepared to plan for projects to be undertaken during the budget year.

According to them the capital budget caters for construction of roads, electrification, schools and hospitals. AEDA prepares Budgeted income statement to summarize all the departmental cash budgets into a single budget called the master budget.

As to whether budgets are approved before implementation respondents who are heads of departments responded that the General Assembly has the sole mandate to approve the final budget during Assembly meetings. They said the budget committee after preparing the budget present it to the General Assembly for discussion and approval, when satisfied with the contents of the budget.

They add that, if the General Assembly is not satisfied with it the budget will be returned to the budget committee for review before sending it to the General Assembly again. In their view this is normal with all budgets. They mention that heads of departments approve their departmental budgets which will be collated into District Assembly master budget. With respect to when budgets are prepared, respondents said it is prepared in the first quarter of the year. Respondents explained that this is preceded by a circulation of memorandum at the end of the financial year that is, December by the budget officer after consultation with the District Coordinating Director (DCD) requesting all functional heads to submit their estimates and proposals, with these estimates yearly budgets are prepared and reviewed monthly by the budget committee and the General Assembly during their monthly meetings.

After all the estimates and proposals have been considered and evaluated, the final budget is sent to General Assembly for approval before the disbursement of funds by the finance department, for the various budgeted activities. Actual performance is compared with budgeted targets and measures taken to forestall future failures variations or deviations. AEDA issues guidelines before budgets are actually formulated. This is a practice at AEDA as the respondents confirmed all departmental activities which are captured in the master budget ceiling is given to work towards that. About 85% of respondents who are involved in budget preparation said they encounter problems during budget preparation. They argue that the budget is only a plan developed in advance prior to the budget period and listed these as the problems in budget preparation

1. They argue that it is difficult to meet requirements in the various departments in terms of experienced personnel, incentives, appropriate inputs from the various departments and computers. They said further that with all these constraints the staff is committed in the discharge of their duties in budget preparation.

2. Poor database for planning and budgeting statistical data collection for planning and budgeting according to 35% of the respondents who are in management is difficult and existing data for planning and budgeting is about 25%   inaccurate. This makes budget formulation quite difficult.

As to whether problems are encountered in budget preparation, 87% of the respondents agreed, whiles 13% did not agree. According to the respondents who agree some of these problems included operational difficulty, low morals and delays. The respondents who did not agree said lack of in-depth knowledge on the budget implementation hampered proper implementation of budgets at the Assembly and various departments. The other reason is that people with expertise were not involved in the implementation of budgets.

As to whether or not there are benefits in preparation and implementation of budgets, respondents revealed that there are numerous benefits which include the fact that budgets help to determine its financial priorities and assess its performance and make judgments.

To the question whether or not AEDA experiences budget deficit, 95% of respondents responded in the affirmative. Reasons assigned by them for this include the fact that there is poor database for planning and budgeting. Existing data from 2011 to 2012 in the Assembly indicate that budgeted revenue for IGFs has been unachievable due to:

1. Inaccurate and inadequate data for budgeting
2. Lack of and inadequate education on financial liabilities of the people to the Assemble.
3. Low financial and non-financial motivation for revenue collectors which leads to revenue leakages.
4. Inadequate logistics' for revenue collection especially where there is only one vehicle for revenue education or even none
5. Lack of proper monitoring and supervision of revenue collectors
6. Dishonesty in revenue collection and accounting.

SOURCES OF REVENUE

Respondents who are members of Management Sub-Committees of the Assembly and revenue officers said that the sources of revenue to the District Assembly are the IGF and the Central Government Transfers, which is made up of the District Assembly Common Fund, Grants-in-Aid and Ceded revenue.

Table6: A table showing IGF for three years

YEARS	BUDGETED	ACTUAL	VARIANCE
2011	4,261,373.12	3,092,399.36	1,168,973.76
2012	8,710,363.32	3,071,191.32	5,639,172.00
2013-2014	7,102,077.30	1,742,861.62	8,844,938.92

Figure 3: A line graph showing IGF for three years

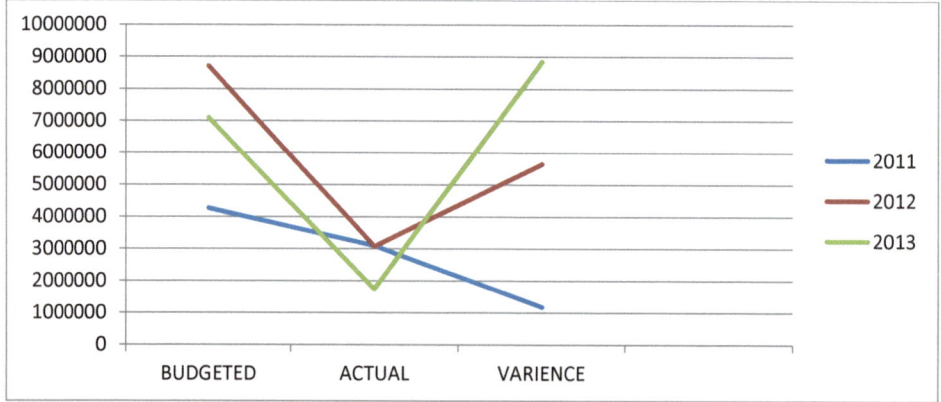

INTERNALLY GENERATED FUND

According to respondents the increase in the year 2011 IGFs was a result of the strategies adopted by the District office to generate revenue which was said to be encouraging as disclosed by the Accountant at the District. When respondents who are District Assembly top Officials were asked on the strategies being adopted to rectify the reduction in the year they mentioned that revenue register had been introduced to ensure effective monitoring of collections to identify defaulters. Available data at the Assembly shows that from the secondary data, basic rate and investment income always perform   poorly whiles land revenue and property rates and licenses perform well because of the nearness of the district to the city.

Table 7: A table showing year-end DACF allocations for three years in Ghana Cedis

CASH FLOW OF DACF ON QUARTERLY BASIS			
QUARTERS	YEAR 2011	YEAR 2012	YEAR 2013
FIRST QUARTERS	47,575.28	2,982,085.00	271,038.00
SECOND QUARTER	92,159.01	77,294.41	207,073.91
THIRD QUARTER	271,515.74	106,121.36	19,157.40
FORTH QUARTER	185,440.44	100,162.64	-
TOTAL	596,690.47	3,265,663.41	497,269.31

Sourse: District Finance Office- cash book

Figure 4: A line graph showing increases in DACF inflows to the Assembly 2011, 2012, 2013-2014

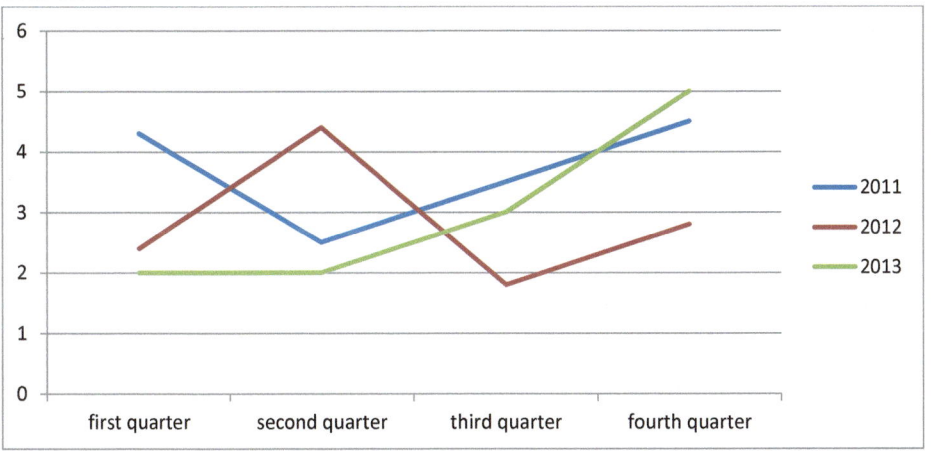

Records at the Assembly show that, the AEDAs share of the Common Fund allocations reduces over the period from 2011-2013. From a total of GH¢596,690.47 in the year 2011 to a total of GH¢3,265,663.41 in the year 2012 and further increase to GH¢ 497,269.31 in the year 2013.

Respondents who are management members stated that increases or decreases in the Common Fund allocation can be explained by changes in years and the government's commitment to fulfilling its part of the development agenda. The District Planning Officer revealed that, the district Assembly benefits from grants and donors such as Community Water and Sanitation Program (CWSP), Social Investment Fund (SIF), Ghana Education Trust Funds (GETFUND), School Feeding Program (SFP), District Development Fund (DDF) Community Based Rural Development Project (CBRDP). These funds from the donors mentioned above do not come from the government but the district solicits from these donors for projects in the districts and these form about 60% of the internally generated funds as the District Accountant revealed. The purpose of this is to remove bureaucracy and delays in implementing government programs at the grassroots level, encourage local   initiatives, empower the local structures to meet their needs and aspirations, and reduce over reliance on central government for development.

BUDGETARY CONTROLS AND PERFORMANCE EVALUATION

As to whether budgetary controls exist in the Assembly, 90% of respondents responded in the affirmative. According to them the guidelines given out to the various budgeted activities responsibilities assigned, resources allocated is an evidence. They explain that after the allocation of the funds to the various activities, the functional heads apply for the release of the funds by writing a memo to the District Coordinating Director (DCD) who is the spending officer. The DCD will then forwards all requests   to the head of finance who will also advise the DCD on how to go about it. The DCD and the head of finance will meet the District Chief Executive (DCE) to discuss the issue in accordance with financial laws of the country such as the Internal Audit Act, the Financial Administration Act and the Public Procurement Act.

To a question as to whether AEDA evaluates budget variance and performance reports, 92% of respondents who are members of AEDA management said it is a common feature about budget implementation. 8% of the respondents were aware that budget variance and performance reports have been evaluated but were not aware of the outcome of evaluated report. For respondents who said that budget variances are evaluated mentioned that it was the responsibility of the budget committee and Finance and Administration (F&A) Sub-Committee to evaluate the budget variance and performance reports. They stated that these bodies are responsible for the formulation, implementation and post implementation of the budget including the evaluation of the budget variance and performance reports.

As to whether or not budget variance and performance reports were of any use to the Assembly, respondents mentioned the following:

1. Evaluate the efficiency of managers in running their departments
2. Improve upon its next period budget
3. To identify a specific problem
4. To shape employees on times of deviations

To the question whether or not managerial sanctions for not meeting targets are imposed, 80% of the respondents revealed that queries are issued out to non-performing managers to explain to the Budget committee and Finance and Administration sub-committee their reason for non-performance. 20% of respondents however said they were not aware if sanctions were imposed on revenue collectors who failed to meet budgeted revenue targets.

As to whether   incentive packages exist for revenue collectors who meet revenue targets, 95% of respondents who are revenue collectors said incentives   like bonus and new assignments are given out to them if they are able to meet or exceed revenue collection targets. To the question as to how are budgetary controls applied at AEDA, respondents who are part of the management, F&A Sub-Committee and budget committee said budgetary controls are applied at AEDA through ;

1. Preparing of a budget on a given format and according to budget guidelines
2. Adherence to budget guidelines and procedures
3. Assigning of responsibilities for proper estimation of revenue and expenditure
4. Allocation of resources according to budget guidelines
5. Checking if expenditure are on course
6. Making continuous comparison of actual results with budget results
7. Checking if departments and Assembly objectives are to be achieved.

REVENUE AND EXPENDITURE

Table   5: A table showing revenue budgets and actuals for the years 2011, 2012, and 2013

Source: Field data, 20th May, 2014

Figure 3: A line graph showing budgeted and actuals of Revenue for the period 2011 to 2013. Documents and records at the Assembly show that, budgeted revenues are higher than actual revenues   resulting in revenue deficit and the district was not able to achieve revenue target for 2011 to 2013. This evidence is shown in the line graph above. According to 90% of the respondents, the reason is that:

I. Revenue was over-estimated without taking into account people ability to pay;

II. Revenue collectors enriched themselves by restoring to fraudulent means

III. As a result of poor performance of the Assembly and its inability to fulfill promises to constituents, payment defaults were high during those years;

IV. Supervision of revenue collection declined because of Management low motivation;

V. Income declined as a result of poor prices of farm products

Respondents who are revenue collectors said revenue targets have not been achieved because, as collectors;

a) Their efforts are not recognized and rewarded
b) They received psychological torture in the form of abuses and insults as well as physical assaults.
c) They are not offered protection against physical assaults and insults
d) They are not given identity (ID) cards or even when they have the ID cards, these are not renewed to empower them to collect revenue.

However, 90% of the respondents were of the view that AEDA has competent personnel as well as competent planning team   to deal with budget and budgetary control issues.

According to them it will be extremely difficult for such personnel to deviate from the objective s of the Assembly. However, 10% of the respondents said that some people who can help in the planning and budgeting processes are not invited to share their ideas.

Table7. REVENUE

YEARS	BUDGETED	ACTUAL
2011	4,261,373.12	3,092,399.36
2012	8,710,363.32	3,071,191.32
2013	7,102,077.30	1,742,861.62

Source: Field data 20th May, 2014

Secondary data at the Assembly show that the budget for expenditure of IGF is always higher than the actual expenditure. The percentage of actual against budgeted expenditure was 72.86%, 37.46% and 15.07% for years 2011, 2012, 2013 respectively. This reveals that the budgeted expenditure for years 2011 and 2013 were less than 50% of their actual meaning.

Table 8 EXPENDITUER

Year	2011	2012	2013	2014
Budgeted	4087788.11	381,612.50	616,624.00	-
Actuals	2978184.81	280,821.81	273,113.94	-

Expenditures are over estimated resulting in surplus or excess revenue. 90% of the respondents related to budgets revealed that these are due to the following:

I. Poor data base for planning and budgeting
II. Poor forecasting abilities

Secondary data at the Assembly (Table 7and 8) shows that the budget for expenditure was less than the budgeted revenue by 4.25%. However the actual expenditure was lower than the budgeted figure which means less was spent in 2011 and excess revenue of 3.84% was experienced. In 2012, more was budgeted for revenue and less for expenditure and the revenue was 4.38% of the expenditure, but with the actuals, more revenue was generated whereas there was 9.14% excess revenue over expenditure. In 2013, budgeted revenue was greater than budgeted expenditure and the percentage of revenue over expenditure was 57.78%. Again, there was excess revenue over expenditure at a rate of 0.59%. From (Table 4), actual revenue in 2011 and 2013 were less than actual expenditure. In all these variances, 85% of the respondents related the causes to:

I. The desire to cut down certain recurrent expenditure such as entertainment feeding of Assembly staff, entertainment of official guest etc.
II. Strict adherence to expenditure rules and procedures;
III. Regular monitoring and evaluation of revenue and expenditure during the period.

SUMMARY OF FINDINGS

The research has revealed how MMDAs formulate, implement and control their budgets and the problems they face in the formulation, implementation and control of their budgets. It was found out that;

1. Respondents selected for this study have knowledge about budgets, budgeting process and implementation

2. The Assembly practices the feedback budgetary controls as it measures the difference between planned and actual results to modify subsequent actions to achieve required results;
3. The Assembly prepares annual budgets at the first quarter of every year and the General Assembly approves the final budgets before implementation;
4. Budgets are very useful as they help the Assembly to determine its financial priorities and assess its performance;
5. Poor database for planning and budgeting, lack of computers, lack of incentives and lack of experienced personnel in the various departments are some of the problems the Assembly encounters in budget preparation and control, operational difficulty, low morale and delays are other problems the Assembly encounters in the budget implementation ;
6. 6. Expenditure guidelines are distributed to the spending officers and other heads of department to show the Assembly's concern for expenditure controls;
7. Measures put in place by the Assembly to address revenue shortfalls in the budget are the following;
i. Incentive packages are given out to revenue collectors who meet or exceed revenue collection targets and this is not frequently done;
ii. Vehicles and logistics are made available for revenue mobilization;
iii. Revenue registers have been introduced to ensure effective monitoring of revenue collection as well as to identify defaulters.

CONCLUSIONS

The following conclusions have been reached based on responses from respondents as well as records and confirmation made available to the research:
1. Budgeting and budgetary controls are management tools of MMDAs for enhancing financial management specially AEDA, this assertion is made because the Assembly prepares budgets, check if expenditures are on course, assigns responsibilities and compares actual results with budgeted results;
2. The Assembly prepares annual, medium-term and long term plans through rigorous processes and procedures which indicate that it attaches importance to planning and Budgeting;
3. AEDA experiences budget deficits because most of its budgeted revenues are less than budgeted expenditure, in some cases this is attributable to poor budgetary controls;
4. AEDA has a budget committee with fourteen (14) members which monitors the preparation, implementation and post implementation of annual budgets;
5. AEDA issues budget guidelines prior to budget preparation and follows the financial laws such as the Public Procurement Act 663 (2003), Internal Audit Act 654 (2003) and the Financial Administration Act 658 (2003) as well as Financial Memorandum for local authorities in preparation and implementation of its annual budgets;
6. There is active participation of all the departments in the budget preparation as every department submits their inputs into the annual budget proposals.
   Departmental heads are invited to budget committee meetings to defend their proposals and this encourages active participation in the budget preparation and implementation at AEDA leading to improve financial performance;

7. Budgeting is one of the fundamental decision making process at AEDA as it serves numerous purposes, as it aids planning, co-ordination, communication, control and performance evaluation. During budget formulation targets are set for each department of the Assembly and the resources required to achieve these targets are estimated.

8. Budgetary controls enhance financial management in MMDA's especially AEDA as they;

i. Eliminate or reduce corruption

ii. ii. Enhance effective revenue mobilization

iii. Share responsibilities

iv. Ensure judicial use of resources

The Assembly attaches much importance to budget and budgetary control as a vital management tool to enhance their financial management.

RECOMMENDATIONS

Based on the findings and conclusions in the research, the following recommendations are made for consideration by AEDA, other MMDAs and the central government.

(a) The Assembly should intensify financial capacity building for revenue collectors, budget officers, Finance and Administration sub-committee members, the Presiding Member and the Management. There is the need for continuous training on budgeting to ensure that officers keep abreast of the new developments in the field of public finance budgeting. It is imperative that there must be capacity building in budget controls at all levels if effectiveness is to be attained. Capacity building should be continuous process and among other things should include how to evaluate budget performance and deal with budget deficits. Training in financial management would ensure that budget control is not regarded as only a management function but as an act of financial discipline.

(b) The Assembly should as a matter of urgency compile an up-to-date register of all ratable items as well as a revaluation of all properties under its jurisdiction. Availability of those registers will eliminate the rampant evasion of payment of property rates. To maintain reliable data on   revenue   sources and rate payers, the District Assembly should have more computers and update its software to effectively help in data processing. There must be prompt prosecution of revenue collectors who embezzle funds collected from taxes, rates, licenses, etc. rate defaulters should also be prosecuted.

(c) The fee fixing resolutions of the Assembly should be published and gazette to have the force of law; a lawyer should be engaged by the Assembly to facilitate prosecution of rate defaulters in court.

(d) The Assembly should explore new revenue sources and should properly manage the traditional sources so as to increase their revenue base in an effort to increase its revenue, auxiliary services like toilet facilities, first aid centers and transit quarters should be provided at the markets and the lorry parks for use by travelers and other people; such auxiliary services could be leased out to the private sector to operate for a share of the proceeds.

(e) Adequate information should be gathered and critically examined using all possible parameters before arriving at budget decision, this will require rigorous appraisal technique and   skills and in order to achieve this, the Assembly should use the services of consultants to assist them plan and prepare good budget.

(f)   Ghana government should collaborate with other Non-governmental organizations to sponsor and award scholarships to students to carry out more research and in-depth studies into budget and budgetary control practices and other relevant financial issues that will benefit the Assemblies.

REFERENCES

Abernethy, M.A., Brownell (1997), Management Control Systems in Research and Development Organizations. The Role of Accounting, behaviour and personnel Controls. Accounting Org. Soc. 22; pp 233-248.Adu-Gyamfi, O. (2008),   Public Sector Financial Management, Accounting and Auditing in Ghana. Pages 139-161 Amoako-Gyampah K. Acquaah M. (2008), "Manufacturing strategy, competitive strategy and firm performance: An empirical study in a developing economy environment",

Production Economics, vol. 3, Issue 2 pp. 575-592. Andrews, M., &Hill, H. (2003), "The Impact of Traditional Budgeting Systems on the Effectiveness of Performance-Based Budgeting: A Different Viewpoint on Recent Findings." International Journal of Public Administration 26, no. 2: pp135 http://www.questia.com/PM.qst?a=o&d=5001905208. Aryee, J.R.A. (1994), An Anatomy of public Policy Implementation – The Case of decentralization Policies in Ghana Aldershot, U.K; Avebury CORE. Aryee, J.R.A. (1999), "Decentralization and the Provision of Local Public Services in Ghana" in Karl Wohlmuth, Hans Bass & Frank Messner (eds.), Good Governance and Economic Development. Public Management,   pp   20.   http://www.questia.com/PM.qst?a=o&d=5000213280.   Financial statement – Ada East District (2011, 2012, 2013). Budget and budgetary control- project work(2011) Anohene Julia

Frederick, D.(2001), "Budgetary control", credit management,ABI/INFORM Global, pp.36

ACCRONYMS AND ABBREVIATIONS

DCD District Co-ordinating Director

DFO District Finance Officer

DBO District Budget Officer

DACF District Assembly Common Fund

MMDAs Metropolitan/Municipal/District Assemblies

IGF Internally Generated Fund

RCC   Regional Co-ordinating Council

F&A Finance and Administration

FAA Finance and Administration Act

FAR Finance and Administration   Regulations

IAA Internal Audit Act

PPA   Public Procurement Act

www.ingramcontent.com/pod-product-compliance
Lightning Source LLC
Chambersburg PA
CBHW041142180526
45159CB00002BB/704